X 1/13 MAY   2012   LAST   CR

CHILDREN'S AUTHORS

NIKKI GRIMES

Jill C. Wheeler

ABDO Publishing Company

visit us at
www.abdopublishing.com

Published by ABDO Publishing Company, 8000 West 78th Street, Edina, Minnesota 55439.
Copyright © 2012 by Abdo Consulting Group, Inc. International copyrights reserved in all
countries. No part of this book may be reproduced in any form without written permission from the
publisher. The Checkerboard Library™ is a trademark and logo of ABDO Publishing Company.

Printed in the United States of America, North Mankato, Minnesota.
062011
092011

PRINTED ON RECYCLED PAPER

Cover Photo: Getty Images
Interior Photos: Getty Images p. 12; Photolibrary p. 15

Photos pp. 5, 7, 9, 11, 17, 18, 19, 21
Copyright © Nikki Grimes
Reprinted by permission of Curtis Brown, Ltd.
All rights reserved

Series Coordinator: Megan M. Gunderson
Editors: Megan M. Gunderson, BreAnn Rumsch
Art Direction: Neil Klinepier

Library of Congress Cataloging-in-Publication Data

Wheeler, Jill C., 1964-
  Nikki Grimes / Jill C. Wheeler.
     p. cm. -- (Children's Authors)
  Includes index.
  ISBN 978-1-61783-047-1
  1. Grimes, Nikki--Juvenile literature. 2. Poets, American--20th century--Biography--Juvenile
literature. 3. African American women poets--Biography--Juvenile literature. I. Title.
  PS3557.R489982Z93 2011
  811'.54--dc22
  [B]
                                      2011010068

CONTENTS

MANY LIVES IN ONE

Nikki Grimes began writing poetry when she was just six years old. Today, she is the author of more than 50 books for children and young adults! Her books often feature her poetry.

Many young readers know Grimes for her popular Danitra Brown books. Many adults are familiar with her work, too. The Southern California Children's Book Association recognized her work with its Golden Dolphin Award in 2005. And in 2006, she received the National Council of Teachers of English Award for Excellence in Poetry for Children.

Grimes says she feels as though she has led many lives. She has traveled the world. And she has been everything from a photographer to a backup singer in a **gospel** act. Many of Grimes's books are based on her own experiences. And many tackle tough themes, such as grief and **foster care**.

Grimes is known for featuring African-American characters. Yet she hopes children of many backgrounds will read her books. She believes books are one of the best ways to learn about other **cultures**.

Grimes says she loves poetry because it can surprise you by touching your heart.

TROUBLED CHILDHOOD

Nikki Grimes was born on October 20, 1950, in Harlem in New York City, New York. Harlem is a historically important African-American neighborhood in the **borough** of Manhattan.

Nikki had an older sister named Carol. Their parents were James and Bernice McMillan Grimes. James was a violinist and a composer. Bernice worked with early computers as a keypunch operator. Sadly, Bernice suffered from **alcoholism** and a mental illness called **paranoid schizophrenia**. She was often in and out of the hospital.

Nikki's parents had a troubled relationship. She remembers them splitting up and then getting back together many times. They separated for good when Nikki was five years old. Soon, she and Carol were separated, too. They were sent to live in different **foster homes**.

Life in the foster-care system was hard for Nikki. She bounced from one foster home to the next. Each meant a

different school and
different friends.
And many were as
troubled as her own
home had been. At
last, she was placed
in a peaceful home in
Ossining, New York.
There, she found a
sense of security she
had never had before.

Nikki's foster brothers in Ossining were Kendall (left) and Brad Buchanan.

FUTURE WRITER

Nikki stayed in Ossining for four years. It was there that she first began to write. Writing stories and poems helped her think about things that were bothering her.

Growing up, Nikki also loved reading. She checked out five or six books at a time from the library. Then, she stayed up late reading them with a flashlight under the covers! There was only one problem. None of the people Nikki read about had a life quite like hers. It made her feel invisible. She vowed to one day write books about kids who looked and felt the way she did.

When Nikki was ten, Bernice remarried. She invited Nikki to live with her again in New York City. Nikki felt torn. She loved her family in Ossining. But, she felt she should be with her mother.

Back in New York City, Nikki moved a lot. At one point, she lived in a rough neighborhood in the **borough** of Brooklyn. Sometimes, she was able to talk her way out of fights. But other times, she couldn't avoid them.

Still, Nikki was a good student and kept up with her reading and writing. Nikki also remained close with her father. He taught her to pay careful attention to the sights and sounds around her. She blended them with her own feelings in her writing.

Then at just 13, Nikki gave her first public poetry reading at Harlem's Countee Cullen Library. And at the end of junior high, she won her first writing award!

Nikki dreamed of one day having her own books on a library shelf.

HIGH SCHOOL CHALLENGES

Young Nikki wasn't just a bookworm, she was also a tomboy! She enjoyed running, swimming, and playing basketball. She even ice-skated on a pair of beautiful white skates her father gave her.

Nikki considered her father to be her best friend and biggest supporter. He bought her books and encouraged her to explore the arts. She even tried playing violin for a while!

After junior high school, Nikki moved to the Bronx. In this New York City **borough**, she attended William Howard Taft High School.

When she was nearly 16, Nikki's world took a tragic turn. Her father suddenly died. The loss made Nikki feel angry and hurt. Worst of all, she felt there was no one she could talk to about her feelings. As she struggled, her grades began to suffer.

Help came in the form of her English teacher Mrs. Evelyn Wexler. She helped Nikki focus on her future. She encouraged Nikki to think about her studies and preparing for college.

As a high school junior, Nikki met another important person. James Baldwin was a successful author with a gift for language. With his guidance and encouragement, Nikki worked to improve her writing and expand her mastery of the English language. In high school, she also published her work for the first time. Her poems appeared in her school's literary journals.

Nikki with her teacher Mrs. Wexler

SEEING THE WORLD

In Sweden, Grimes has been described as a singer who also writes!

After graduating from high school, Grimes did not enter college right away. Instead, she joined a writing group at Columbia University in New York City. There, she met many other writers and learned new skills to apply to her own work.

Two years later, Grimes entered Livingston College at Rutgers University in New Jersey. There, she studied writing with many working poets and other artists. Most important, she learned how to capture the reader's attention in the very first paragraph.

Grimes graduated from Rutgers in 1974 with a degree in English literature. She had also studied African languages, which helped her win a special **grant**. This allowed her to study languages in Tanzania for a year. Her time there inspired her book *Is It Far to Zanzibar?*, which was published in 2000.

After Tanzania, Grimes worked in photography and radio. While producing a children's show on WBAI FM in New York, she met noted author Julius Lester. He became another important mentor. Also during this time, Grimes began getting her work published. Her work was published first in magazines and literary journals, and eventually in books.

Grimes's first children's book, *Growin'*, came out in 1977. It was illustrated by Charles Lilly. The book focuses on friendship, which was an important issue in Grimes's own childhood. Grimes's first book of children's poems, *Something on My Mind*, came out the next year. Also in 1978, Grimes moved to Sweden for a time. She worked in radio and as a translator.

EXPLORING THE ARTS

Grimes returned to the United States in 1984 to work as a **freelance** writer and editor. She then took a job as a library assistant with the University of California, Los Angeles (UCLA). Then in 1989, she became a writer and editor with the Walt Disney Company. Since 1991, she has been a full-time freelance writer.

Writing is just one of Grimes's creative interests. She has published and exhibited her photography. She has made beautiful beaded jewelry and sold it around the United States. And, she has crafted cards from recycled materials.

While in Sweden, Grimes had discovered a passion for knitting and an appreciation for weaving. So in 1999, she published a book about weaving. *Aneesa Lee & the Weaver's Gift* won a Parents' Choice Award. The book blends 13 poems with the steps of weaving such as making dyes, spinning yarn, preparing the loom, and weaving **tapestry**.

Grimes was a library assistant at
UCLA from 1986 to 1988.

Touchy Subjects

Grimes kept her promise to write stories about what mattered to her as a child. Sometimes that meant writing about painful things.

Jazmin's Notebook mirrors Grimes's early life in many ways. It tells the story of a young girl in 1960s Harlem who struggles with everything from teasing to **foster homes**. Young Jazmin conquers these challenges through making friends, writing poetry, and keeping a journal. The book earned a **Coretta Scott King Award Honor** in 1999.

Grimes used her own high school as the setting for *Bronx Masquerade*. The book tells the story of a group of students who do open-mike poetry readings. Their poems offer clues to the difficult issues in their lives. *Bronx Masquerade* won the 2003 Coretta Scott King Author Award.

What is Goodbye? is about two children dealing with the death of their older brother. Grimes tells the story in 26 paired poems. She had a hard time finding a publisher who wanted to tackle such a tough topic. But, the book went on to win many awards. In 2004, it was named an American Library Association (ALA) Notable Book.

Not all of Grimes's characters are make-believe. *Talkin' About Bessie* features African-American **aviator** Bessie Coleman. In 2003, the book became a **Coretta Scott King Author Honor Book** and an ALA Notable Book.

THE PRESIDENT'S STORY

In December 2007, one of Grimes's publishers asked her to write a picture book **biography**. It would be about Illinois senator and presidential candidate Barack Obama.

Award-winning artist Bryan Collier created the illustrations for Grimes's Barack Obama book.

Grimes hesitated because she was very busy. Most picture books took her three to six months to write. Yet she had to research and write the first **draft** for this book in just three weeks! Timing was not the only challenge. Most characters in Grimes's books are children themselves. This time, she had to feature an adult character without losing the interest of her readers.

Grimes chose a **unique** format for the book. She wrote a story within a story. A young African-American boy named David asks his mother to tell him about Obama. Obama's life unfolds through Grimes's poetry. This allowed Grimes to share Obama's story as seen through the eyes of a young person.

The project was exciting for Grimes. When she was young, having an African-American president seemed like an impossible dream. She hoped her book would inspire young readers. She especially wanted to reach out to those who were African-American or who came from single-parent families.

Barack Obama: Son of Promise, Child of Hope went on to spend several weeks at the top of the New York Times Bestseller List. It also received an award from the **NAACP**.

WRITING AND MORE

In addition to writing, Grimes works with her agent, writes to editors, and answers mail from young fans. She also does lots of interviews with magazines, radio stations, and newspapers. And, she keeps her Web site up to date.

Grimes often visits schools and conferences to give lectures. She can be preparing four different events at any one time. Grimes also takes time to speak up in support of libraries, which helped her so much as a child.

Grimes also helps other writers improve their skills. And, she judges literary competitions. Once, she read 105 books for just one contest!

Of course, Grimes also keeps writing! She writes at her home in Corona, California. When she's not working, Grimes enjoys long walks, knitting, reading, talking with friends, cooking, and playing word games. Somehow, she finds time to do it all!

Grimes likes to write by hand and then type what she's written into a computer.

GLOSSARY

alcoholism - a disorder in which a person cannot control his or her urge to drink alcohol.

aviator - a person who operates aircraft.

biography - the story of a real person's life written by someone other than that person.

borough (BUHR-oh) - one of five divisions of New York City. They are Manhattan, the Bronx, Queens, Brooklyn, and Staten Island.

Coretta Scott King Award - an annual award given by the American Library Association. It honors African-American authors and illustrators whose work reflects the African-American experience. Runners-up are honor books.

culture - the customs, arts, and tools of a nation or a people at a certain time.

draft - an early version or outline.

foster care - a system that provides supervision and a place to live outside a person's regular home. A foster home is a place where someone in foster care lives.

freelance - relating to an artist or author without a long-term commitment to a single employer.

gospel - of or relating to religious American music containing elements of folk songs and blues.

grant - a gift of money to be used for a special purpose.

NAACP - National Association for the Advancement of Colored People. The NAACP works toward fairness in housing, employment, education, voting, transportation, and other areas, especially relating to race.

paranoid schizophrenia (PEHR-uh-noyd skiht-suh-FREE-nee-uh) - a mental disorder marked by seeing or hearing things that are not there and believing that people are watching or talking about oneself.

tapestry - a heavy woven fabric decorated with detailed designs or pictures.

unique - being the only one of its kind.

To learn more about Nikki Grimes, visit ABDO Publishing Company online. Web sites about Nikki Grimes are featured on our Book Links page. These links are routinely monitored and updated to provide the most current information available.
www.abdopublishing.com

INDEX